HOME BIRD

FOUR SEASONS
ON MARTHA'S VINEYARD

Essays by Laura Wainwright

Illustrations by J. Ann Eldridge

VINEYARD STORIES
Edgartown, Massachusetts

Published by Vineyard Stories
52 Bold Meadow Road
Edgartown, Massachusetts 02539
508-221-2338
www.vineyardstories.com

Many of these essays first appeared in the *Martha's Vineyard Times*.

Library of Congress Number: 2011944252
ISBN: 978-0-9827146-8-3

Book Design: Jill Dible, Atlanta, Georgia
Editor: Jan Pogue

Printed in China

For Whit, Sam, and Lila, with love

THE RED WHEELBARROW

So much depends
upon

a red wheel
barrow

glazed with rain
water

beside the white
chickens.

—William Carlos Williams

CONTENTS

SUMMER

EVENING WATCH

Even on summer evenings I don't often linger outside. I'll walk down to the beach and take a swim, but once I hang my wet suit on the line and step into the kitchen, this room becomes the center of my concentration. I flick on the lights, turn up the radio, and start dinner.

One of the kids or a guest may call me out onto the back porch to admire the sunset, but no matter how lovely it is, my attention remains with the meal on the stove. The ding of a timer or the scent of finely chopped basil tugs me back inside. So I usually miss the time when light slowly fades and so many animals become active.

Not this evening. Tonight I am home alone. I pour a glass of cold white wine, drag a chair into the far corner of our porch and sink into it. The cottage next door is empty of its usual summer tenants. There are no sing-song voices playing hide and seek in the small yard. No screen doors bang. The grill sits unlit. The porch light is off. I notice three catbirds hopping along the low stone wall between our house and theirs. The undiluted quiet is a gift.

Fog blankets the dropping sun. This isn't one of those nights with wild reds and oranges swirling across the sky. The fading light is the dusty color of a blueberry. As the dusk slowly ebbs, I watch the color bleed and thicken to a deep plum against the umber of the newly mown field.

A tawny smudge moves at the bottom of the field, catching my eye. I wait. Out from behind a huckleberry bush steps a young doe. Her four legs are delicate and lanky, thin strips of gold against a puddle of the blue grey light. She must sniff me, since she stops and looks my way, but she does not startle. Instead, she twists to rub her hind leg with her head, indulging in a long, thorough scratch before continuing along the path.

I can't count the number of times I've watched my own children and dogs meander down this same trail heading for the beach. I anticipate where she will vanish behind two beetlebungs and then move my eyes to the exact spot where she will reappear. I track her journey until she disappears at the far end of the field, absorbed by a purple patch of oak.

Just as I lose sight of the deer, two skunks saunter into view as if on cue. Separated solely by a low stone wall, these solitary animals seem oblivious of one another. What innate signal roused them from their burrows at the exact same moment? One patrols our yard, while the other commandeers the cottage field. They notice me: both tails are up in warning, but otherwise they sniff the ground for grubs, fully absorbed with the business of dinner.

Their black-and-white coats look glossy and thick. The white stripe glows iridescent in the advancing dark. I have an urge to run my hand through their fur, but it's short-lived. The skunk in our yard comes closer and closer to my perch on the porch. He's more at home than I am comfortable with. I click my tongue to remind him I'm here. It works. He races across the lawn and slithers over the wall and vanishes in a tangle of bittersweet and wild cherry.

Stars pepper the sky. It's fully dark now, and the thought of my own dinner pulls me inside. Encircled by the yellow glow of my cozy kitchen I try to picture all the other animal lives I run parallel to but rarely intersect with. Who else do I routinely miss? Otters? Owls? Raccoons? Moles? Spiders? I wonder how many species use the path I think of as ours and which animals are just now getting up and starting their day in the night?

I'm grateful to be reminded of the extraordinary way living things fill each niche. It's too easy to forget how remarkably complex and rich our world is. From the kitchen window I can just make out the outline of my bathing suit on the line. Tomorrow morning when I put it on, I'll be following the deer's path to the beach and looking for signs of other travelers. Tomorrow evening I hope to be back on the porch watching and listening to the vibrant world that's always there. It's just a matter of paying attention.

FIRST POTATOES

The large flat potato fields of eastern Long Island stretching from narrow roads to ocean dunes were central to my childhood landscape in the fifties. My father's summer cottage was next to a potato field. Potatoes were the first crop I ever harvested. At dinnertime, Dad would put a pot of water on to boil and send me out into the fields to dig. He told me he had the farmer's permission, but I never really knew, and I vowed someday I'd grow my own.

I had to wait until the late seventies for my own garden, but finally I was able to share one in Chilmark with a friend. Potatoes were the crop I most wanted to grow. I dedicated a whole row to potatoes within our deer-fenced garden. We had a ten-pound bag of potatoes that had sprouted, so I didn't even bother to buy seed. I cut the spuds into nuggets, making sure each piece had a few eyes, and then let them scar up on an old screen over our bathtub. In a few days they were ready for planting.

Many people put the seed potatoes right on the ground and cover them with straw, but I wanted to plant them the way the farmers in Long Island did. I dug a shallow trench, lined it with manure, and placed the seed potatoes about twelve inches apart. Then I covered them over with hay. These potatoes were generous. As they sprouted and grew, I filled in around the plants with dirt and hay, but other than giving them an occasional boost of manure tea, I waited.

My hope was to harvest the potatoes on the Fourth of July when our family held an annual baseball game and cookout at our camp near the Brickyards. I wanted to make James Beard's simple potato salad for our friends and family. Thrusting my hands into the warm, friable soil, I felt gently under the plants and took just the biggest potatoes. I knew if I was careful the plant would survive and more potatoes could develop. I'm a visual person, so depending on touch was a new and delicious sensation. That year the salad was small, but I moved the potatoes to another spot, unfenced, and in later years grew enough for lots of salads.

This year I didn't plant my own potatoes, but today I got lucky. My neighbor and friend Debby Farber of Blackwater Farm knows how I feel about potatoes. This morning she called and invited me to help her dig her first baby potatoes for the Farmer's Market tomorrow. I went right over.

Debby led the way down the rows using a pitchfork to loosen the dirt around the plants. Her helper, Kit Luckey, and I had the fun of following behind. We pulled away the plants, picked off all the small potatoes still attached to them, and dug deep into the soft brown earth with our hands to gather up any strays.

Each row had different varieties of potatoes, and we picked four kinds of early varieties: Red Gold, Superior, Mountain Rose and Yukon Gold. Soon we filled two big buckets with the precious nuggets. The potatoes were small, ranging in size from a hazelnut to a large walnut. The Red Gold, which can be recognized by the yellow color under the delicate red skin, are my favorites. Debby insisted I fill two one-pound boxes and take them home. I would cook them for dinner.

Rinsing the potatoes in my kitchen sink, all thoughts of waiting evaporated. These potatoes would be at their best this very moment. I put off a couple of things I'd planned to do and put the newly dug, freshly washed potatoes in a large pot of salted water to boil.

James Beard's potato salad, adapted from the writer Alexandre Dumas, is simple. I know it by heart. Sitting outside in the shade half an hour later, I ate the whole bowlful. Each bite made me happy.

Alexandre Dumas Potato Salad
by James Beard
4–6 SERVINGS

Ingredients:
4–6 good-sized potatoes, preferably the waxy or new type
Salt and pepper to taste
$1/2$ cup olive oil
$1/2$ cup dry white wine
1 tablespoon vinegar
$1/2$ cup chopped parsley
$1/2$ cup chopped chives or green onions

Boil potatoes in their skins until you can just pierce them with a knife. Peel while hot, and slice into a bowl. Season with salt and pepper to taste, and add the olive oil and white wine. Stir gently to combine. Let the potatoes cool and just before serving, toss them with the vinegar, parsley, chives or green onions and additional salt if you'd like.

FORAGING: DO IT GENTLY

In the autumn of 1978, I came to Martha's Vineyard to visit a new boyfriend at the camp he had built in Chilmark near the Brickyards. We spent the weekend fishing off Noman's Land, raking up clams in Menemsha Pond, and picking enough wild grapes from his yard to make a pie. I fell in love with the man, the place, and foraging.

I started with fruit. The woods around his camp were full of blueberry and huckleberry bushes. Blackberry stalks and grapevines sprawled abundantly alongside the dirt road, and beach plums grew in the shadow of the Brickyard chimney. If I could avoid the poison ivy and Preston Harris's cows grazing among the ruins, the plums were mine for the picking.

Over time I expanded to other foods. Friends showed me where to collect hazelnuts on Peaked Hill and took me to a secret spot to gather watercress in the spring. At low tide, we'd scour rocks along the North Shore, picking up the feathery seaweed hoping to find mussels underneath. We'd rake for oysters in Tisbury Great Pond and scallops and cherrystones in Menemsha Pond. In September we'd keep our crab nets and buckets in the car in case we had a chance to stop at Chilmark Pond or Crab Creek at Quansoo.

High summer often found me deep in a secret thicket of highbush blueberries, with a baby on my back and a coffee can on a string around my neck. At first the berries pinged against the metal of the can, but soon the sound thickened to a quiet, satisfying plop. I'd make jams and coffee cakes and put bags of blueberries into the freezer hoping to capture the season's essence. Blueberries smell like summer as they thaw.

I am still an active forager, but in comparison to the younger generation, my foraging is modest, plebian really. I stick with shellfish, berries, and a few easily recognized mushrooms. This year, out of curiosity and for fun, I decided to try something different and see what I could forage right from my own back yard in Lambert's Cove. Our lot, just over an acre in size, is a mixture of grass and trees.

The results so far are mixed. There are plenty of dandelion greens, but I find them bitter. Tiny green grapes are swelling on a vine that is climbing our huge Norway spruce. With luck there may be enough for a batch of spiced wild grape jelly. I've been ambivalent about the Russian olive that invaded our yard, but thanks to a recent Wild Food Challenge I now know I can make a delicious sorbet with its berries or mix them with other fruits into a crumble. Chestnuts are ripening on our lone American chestnut tree, and after the last rain I found a few puffballs on the lawn. After I finish writing today, I'll check to see if there are any remaining blackberries in the thicket behind the garage.

No purist, I have no intention of limiting my foraging to our yard. We have no blueberries or huckleberries, so I've been gathering them at Blackwater Preserve. In mid-August I wandered the trails with my two great nieces, grazing as we walked. Our baggie was still empty when we came home, but our fingers were stained deep purple, and our bellies were content.

With so many of us gathering wild foods, it's important that we forage with sensitivity — mindful of how much we take and what our impact is. When taking fish and game, including shellfish, we need to respect legal limits. We should only pick things that are renewable and pick in moderation. It is one thing to collect for personal use and quite another to pick a large quantity for profit. Last summer the beach plums came early and they were plentiful. I picked a small bucket to make a batch of jelly for my family. On my way home I passed a man lugging two five-gallon buckets overflowing with beach plums, one in each hand. It seemed greedy. Let's each of us commit to foraging responsibly, keeping it fun, and remembering to share.

Spiced Wild Grape Jelly
MAKES ABOUT 12 JELLY GLASSES

4 quarts wild grapes, removed from stems
1 pint vinegar
$1/4$ cup whole cloves
$1/4$ stick of cinnamon, broken up
3 pounds sugar (approximately)

Do not wash grapes. Place in a large kettle, crush with a potato masher, add vinegar and spices. Mix and crush again. Cook mixture 15 minutes over medium heat. Let sit overnight. Dip liquid out carefully, leaving sediment on the bottom. Measure juice and sugar, cup for cup. Heat to boiling, stirring sugar to help dissolve it. Cook until jelly sheets from a spoon. Cool slightly, skim, and pour into clean hot containers. Seal at once.

Adapted from *The Martha's Vineyard Cookbook: A Diverse Sampler from a Bountiful Island* by Louise Tate King and Jean Stewart Wexler, 1971.

RASPBERRY PICKING

"Raspberries" is written in red on the hand-painted sign in front of Mermaid Farm, but you'll only see it if you are driving down Island on Middle Road. Heading up Island, I missed the good news, but fortunately I pulled into the farm anyway.

I stop at Mermaid Farm whenever I pass by. The farm stand is one of the best on the Island, and it's a pleasure to make a selection of Caitlyn Jones's heirloom tomatoes and then walk up to the dairy barn and buy the raw milk and thick, rich yogurt made by her husband, Allen Healy.

Pulling in and parking by the farm stand, I saw I was smack in front of a huge raspberry patch. Raspberries are my favorite fruit, and I love to pick them. How had I missed this before? There were no picked berries for sale, but a sign with clear instructions was posted next to the price list:

PICK YOUR OWN RASPBERRIES

You need to find and speak to me first
$4/pint

1. Do not hurt/bother the spiders or bees
2. No walking perpendicular to the rows

This sounded just right. I liked being warned not to look out for the bees and spiders harming me but my possible impact on their well-being. I walked to the house to ask Caitlyn for permission, hoping she was home and that I would pass muster. Before I got to the door she opened a window? "Yes?"

"Can my daughter and I pick raspberries?"

"Go for it!"

We entered the patch carefully, watching more for spiders and bees than for brambles. Could we resist the temptation to taste? No. The berries tasted like an Indian summer day, sweet and tart at the same time. Embraced by the hum of bees, we began to pick.

Each stalk we examined was laden with berries in all stages of ripeness. We moved — not perpendicularly — down the rows, for the pleasure of it, not because we needed to. It took no time to fill our pint containers, but I lingered over mine to savor the abundance of all that lovely fruit and admire the enormous spiders and their intricate webs.

The picking was so satisfying that I came back later that afternoon with a friend. This time Allen's father, Kent Healy, was picking. "You know you have to pick them every day," he reminded us. Raspberries are delicate. It's one of the things I like about them. They need to be eaten right away or they spoil. This meant I would need to come back the next day – just what I wanted to do anyway.

A hoarder, I had been looking at cookbooks and thinking I needed to make jam or put away some raspberry vinegar for Christmas presents. I told Kent this as we picked. His response was just what I needed and wanted to hear, "Aw, just eat them. They're never better than fresh."

How true. I came home and poured most of the pint I picked into a huge bowl, buried it in Allen's whole milk yogurt, and drizzled honey on top. I sat outside in a patch of afternoon sun with the *Joy of Cooking*, turning back and forth from the page on how to freeze raspberries to the page on how to make cheesecake. How good would a lemon cheesecake topped with fresh raspberries be? Excellent.

Today I'll go back to Mermaid Farm and pick again. There is a metaphor about picking just the right berry that I'm trying to wrap my mind around, and it may take quite a few pints before I get a handle on it. Why is it that unripe berries resist a gentle tug so you leave them behind while the overripe ones fall into your hand too easily, leaving a stain? Raspberries that are just right require only a tiny touch of pressure and they rest between your fingers intact and perfect. They give themselves to you.

The message, I believe, is something about being patient and letting things happen in their own time. Somewhere in there is something about enjoying things at their peak, but I will need to go back and pick and pick again before I really get it. Only one thing is certain: finding out will be a pleasure.

RENTING TO AN OLD BOYFRIEND

Our place is a little tricky to rent. For starters, we have a few brown bats in the basement. These days there are people who don't like to go down to a cellar to do their laundry. We're a softer generation. Even fewer like to go down to a cellar with bats swooping through it at night. I mean, they do keep the bugs down, but how do you explain that?

And then there are the ticks and the poison ivy. Should I tell a prospective renter they need to look out for these things? Will they be amused when I mention that my father-in-law once called this place Griswold's Tick Ranch and Poison Ivy Farm? I don't think so.

So I hope people look beyond the furniture, well worn is a nice term, and the floors, a bit soft in places, to the view, which is spectacular. This is the kind of place that could only have been bought for a song in the 1930s when Lamberts Cove was considered the hinterland by down-Islanders. It was, and since then the house has been in my husband's family, which is how we have it and also why we need to rent it to stay in it. We are the downwardly mobile, which gets me back to renting.

This year we tried to strike a middle ground with the whole rental thing. Not ask the biggest buck, despite the nearby beach and the water view, and not have to replace the furniture and the floors. So I started with our friends and sent out a general email.

I got lots of advice — use a realtor, charge more, charge less, stay home — but no prospective customers. Still the word was out there so I decided to just be patient and let the chips fall where they may, and the right thing would happen. Then the phone rang.

I didn't recognize the voice. "I hear you may be renting your house. It's Jamie, Jamie Childs." I was not prepared for this. Jamie was my first boyfriend, and we had lived together for more than three years. I'd died for that voice once, and now I didn't recognize it. Miracles happen.

The email had somehow reached him. He wanted to come to the Island and fish and bring his son and his new girlfriend and her boys. The apple was falling right next to the tree after thirty years — plenty of time, but did I want him sleeping in my bed?

I remembered the bats and laughed. Jamie and I had studied bats together in college. Twice we'd gone to Jamaica to collect bats for a research project. Perfect. He would think the bats were a plus. I knew he'd gone on to be a scientist and after working at the Centers for Disease Control on the Ebola virus was now at Yale doing something similar.

"There are a few bats in the basement."

"Really! What kind?"

It might work. We agreed on a price and a time and I even got him to agree to look after our pets. I just had to clean everything and get used to inviting that old energy back into my life. It all felt a bit odd, but I didn't hesitate to cash his check when it came.

Now the time has come and he arrives Thursday. We spoke today to arrange the final details. I haven't seen the bats lately, and I'm worried they fell prey to whatever is killing bats all over New England. I decided not to mention it. I didn't want to disappoint him.

As our conversation was wrapping up, Jamie asked me about ticks. Oh God, I thought, here we go. "Well, of course we have them, but they don't seem to be that bad this year. You just need to check yourself. It's not really a big deal."

"Oh, that's too bad. I was hoping for a big crop. I've invited some scientists down from Yale who want to collect ticks."

This might be a perfect match.

STRIPED BASS

On Labor Day the whole Island exhaled, and for the first time all summer my husband and I went for a ride in his boat. When we met thirty-five years ago Whit was a charter guide out of Menemsha, and much of our early courtship involved being on the water together. Then came two children, a slew of pets, and, of course, work. Time on the water became a memory.

But today we packed a picnic, rowed out to his boat on a mooring in Lambert's Cove, and climbed aboard. I wanted to do something new, something we'd never done before, so instead of steaming west toward Gay Head as usual, we turned east and headed for Chappaquiddick. Just off Makonikey we saw lots of terns and gulls bunched up and diving. Stopping, we saw a patch of water churning with fish.

I love watching my husband on a boat — setting the drift, tying on a popping plug, and sending out that first cast. He had a hit as soon as he started reeling in. The rod doubled over. Because of its strong, frantic fight, we assumed the fish was a blue, but when it was close enough to the boat to see clearly, we saw he had caught a lovely striper. The bass measured a full twenty-nine inches — a keeper, and into the fish box it went.

Continuing on to Chappy we explored Edgartown harbor and picnicked in Cape Pogue Bay. After lunch Whit carefully cleaned and skinned the striper before heading home. The ride was wet but fun and gave me time to think about how to prepare the fillets. The beauty and spirit of a bass is particularly humbling, so when we catch one I want to honor it by cooking it really well. The treatment would depend on the weather. September is mercurial, so I would have to wait and see.

The next day was still summery, so I decided to broil one of the fillets using a simple treatment from Mark Bittman's *How to Cook Everything*. Setting the broiler at 450 degrees, I preheated a cast iron pan for five minutes before adding a few tablespoons of butter and olive oil and a salted skinless fillet. I put the pan back under the broiler for four minutes on one side, then flipped the fish and cooked it for three minutes on the other. This is less time than Bittman suggested but was perfect for the thickness of our fillet. We squeezed fresh lemon juice on it and ate it with a corn and black bean salad I'd made earlier that day and a big handful of baby arugula.

The warm weather did not last. The following morning a cool rain fell. I put on a sweater for the first time in months and never took it off. Instead of opening windows and doors, I closed them. That evening it made sense to cut up the other bass fillet and cook it in a thick white bean and tomato stew flavored with bacon and saffron. This is one of my favorite preparations for striped bass. The original recipe from *Bon Appetit* calls for halibut, but striped bass makes an excellent substitution.

That evening, with the addition of a loaf of crispy French bread, a green salad, and a bottle of dry white wine, we had a wintery meal worthy of this magnificent fish. Two fillets. Two seasons. Both delicious.

White Bean and Striped Bass Stew

4–6 SERVINGS

4 thick-cut bacon slices, chopped
1 cup sliced shallots
3 tablespoons extra virgin olive oil
6 garlic cloves, chopped
1 can petite diced tomatoes in juice, $14^{1}/_{2}$-ounce
1 bottle clam juice, 8-ounce
$^{1}/_{2}$ cup dry white wine
$^{1}/_{2}$ teaspoon saffron threads
2 cans small white beans drained, 15-ounces each
$1^{1}/_{2}$ pounds striped bass fillets, cut into $1^{1}/_{2}$-inch chunks
chopped parsley to taste

Sauté bacon and shallots in large, heavy-bottomed pot over medium high heat until bacon is crisp — about 7 minutes. Add olive oil and garlic; stir 1 minute. Add tomatoes with juice, clam juice, wine, and saffron and bring to boil. Reduce heat; simmer 5 minutes. Add beans and fish; bring to simmer. Cover and simmer until fish is just opaque in center — about 5 minutes. Season to taste with salt and pepper. Add fresh parsley.

SWIMMING

Wet bathing suits are back on the line, and we shower outside amid pale pink roses that tangle in my hair. We brush by the fireplace in our rush to get outside, barely recalling its central place in our lives these past six months. Summer solstice is just two days away, and now we're eating barefoot on the porch and listening to screen doors slap.

More visitors arrive every day. Hummingbirds have been dashing to the feeder since early May. Catbirds and bluebirds have nested, and the first eggs have already hatched. A friend tells me that when I hear the catbirds sing, I am listening to mothers and babies calling back and forth, trying to strike the right balance. Too much calling and they will attract predators. Too little and the babies might get lost.

Our phone, quiet in March and April, starts ringing off the hook in June. "We're here on the Island, can you come to dinner?" "Can we visit you for three or four nights?" Like the catbirds, finding the right balance can be delicate. Too many guests and we feel like we're running a hotel. Too few and we feel selfish, hoarding this thick summer beauty.

It's hard to set limits when a niece travels all the way from Singapore to visit or a friend from elementary school days wants to drop by. Saying no when the fecund world is shouting yes is a challenge. Even the days are deliciously lopsided with long days of seemingly endless light and short nights punctured early by vibrant birdsong.

What helps me rebalance in these hectic summer months is a good swim each day. Morning plunges start in early June when the water is bracing and cold. Diving in takes my breath away, but I sputter to the surface exhilarated to be here doing this once again. As the water gradually warms, a dip becomes a long, leisurely swim in the shallow waters of Lambert's Cove. I drop a towel on the beach and swim west to the inlet of James Pond and back. The water is so clear I sometimes see striped bass swimming nearby. Occasionally water and movement and beauty create an alchemy that is the closest I get to rapture.

Today I swam in Ice House Pond to remind myself that this delicious alternative is always available. When beach parking lots fill to bursting and visitors outnumber us ten to one, I often leave our wide-open saltwater rim to the summer guests and turn inland.

A tiny Land Bank property off Lambert's Cove Road, the access to Ice House Pond has space for only four cars. It is an ideal place for a quiet swim. Songbirds, flowering blueberries, and stands of oak and evergreen circle the small body of water. Swimming here can be a relief after the challenge of the open sea. Little fish with flashes of blue green on their fins feed on the sandy bottom, their backs dappled by sunlight. Diving in, I braced myself for the sting of salt, but my eyes opened easily in the fresh water. I drank some. It had a loamy sweet taste. My body was heavier in this fresh water, and instead of being buoyed, I felt embraced.

Picking up a languid crawl, I swam to the middle of the pond. Voices of two other swimmers drifted over the spun sugar fog as they called to one another like catbirds. Suddenly it was quiet, and I was alone. I floated on my back and soaked in the magnificent wide sky. The tensions of this season drained away in the cool water. By the time I got out and dripped dry on the metal dock, I had fallen back in love with this Island, with summer solidly fixed on our glorious dizzy planet. At home with a lighter step, I stood in the warm grass and pinned my bathing suit to the clothesline. The catbirds were calling to and fro in the thicket nearby.

It's all about finding the right balance.

YANKEE BONANZA

This spring the beach plum blossoms were magnificent. From the top of the dune near our house, the beachscape was a haze of peachy white. Each branch of every beach plum shrub was laden with flowers that managed to hold on through heavy spring rains. Throughout the summer, I kept a close eye on the beach plum growth. In June the bushes were covered with lots of green fruit. Then in July we had a long period without rain, and it seemed the fruit might not ripen. This past week, however, the fruit rapidly changed from green to red and purple. Each day brought changes. The fruit was ripe, and it was ripe now.

But beach plums aren't ripe in early August. A late summer fruit, I associate picking them with Labor Day and the return to school. I refused to believe what my eyes were seeing because the timing was so off. It took meeting someone on the beach path carrying a full bucket of beach plums to knock some sense into me.

Had I been wrong all these years about the timing? I checked *Plum Crazy: A Book about Beach Plums,* published in 1973 by Elizabeth Post Mirel, my source for everything about this native species. The book is a compendium of beach plum information and lore. It includes botany, history, recipes, beauty products, even information about whittling with beach plum wood and making liquors. Mirel states clearly: "The beach plum ripens from late August to early October. It can be small as a pea or as large as a crabapple. The color of the ripe fruit ranges from red to purple to black and even includes yellow. Take your pick."

I put down the book, found a small bucket, and headed down to the beach. My Yankee roots like the satisfaction of having something wild for free, that you work for. Another more hedonistic part of me enjoys what feels like pure magic — the wonder that a fruit so densely flavorful and tart can emerge out of the sand. Sitting in the warm sand, just across the dune from afternoon beach-goers, I picked until my pail was full.

As I picked, I visualized the yellowed handwritten recipe for beach plum jelly that my mother gave me years ago. She got the recipe from her friend Diana Walker, who picked plums on Tuckernuck, the small island off the west end of Nantucket. Mrs. Walker made the best beach plum jelly I've ever tasted.

Whenever I looked at Mrs. Walker's handwriting, so like my mother's, I was reminded of picking beach plums with Mom at the Brickyards in Chilmark on an early September afternoon in the early 1980s. We hung coffe cans around our necks on rawhide laces to hold our harvest. The pleasurable plunk of plums hitting the can punctuated our conversation as we picked and chatted. Tonight I would finally make this jelly myself.

When I came back from the beach I rinsed the sand off the beach plums and took an outdoor shower. The alchemy of capturing a summer's day in a small Ball jar began. I removed small leaves and twigs but didn't pick off each and every stem. I put the plums into a large stainless steel pot and covered them just enough water to keep them from sticking to the bottom. Soon the kitchen was saturated with the hot dense smell of boiling beach plums. By the end of the evening (I was too impatient to let the juice drip overnight) my pantry was full of tiny jars of beach plum jelly ready to give for gifts or to enjoy.

Once again Yankee roots rubbed up against wonder. Part of me wanted to save and hoard these treasures and another part wanted to open a jar and eat it right then and there. Fortunately a friend stopped by and together we sat outside on the porch and savored a whole jar of the tart burgundy jelly with a cup of strong tea. I served it on wheat thins spread with cream cheese, just the way my mother used to. The jelly tasted as extraordinary as my memory of it. The mixture of sweet and sour captured the fleeting essence of a late summer's day and even the tang of the star we saw streaking across the sky.

Mrs. Walker's Beach Plum Jelly

The best beach plums are those that are not too ripe.

Boil whatever amount you pick in a large kettle, putting in enough water so that there is about three inches in the bottom of the pot.

Bring to a boil and then simmer, stirring frequently and mashing until fruit is separated from the seeds — about 30 minutes. Strain through a jelly bag or cheesecloth into a large bowl. For the most flavorful jelly let it drip overnight. Don't squeeze bag unless you want cloudy jelly.

Next day, measure an equal amount of sugar and juice into a large pot. Boil vigorously for 10 minutes or so and then apply the spoon test: take a spoonful of jelly, cool a moment, then pour back into pot from side of spoon. At first two large drops will form on each side of spoon. When jelly is ready, these drops will come together and sheet off the spoon.

AUTUMN

BAY SCALLOPS

As soon as the family scallop season opens in Chilmark on October 1, my husband digs in the garage for his wooden culling board and the scallop drags I gave him one year for Christmas. He hoses off a pair of wire baskets, loads everything into his truck, and we head for Menemsha harbor where he keeps his boat. We're going scalloping.

Not much is grander than steaming up Menemsha Pond on a shiny autumn morning cradling a hot cup of coffee from the gas dock. The sun dances off the water, and the weather is often still warm enough for just a tee-shirt.

Except for the fishermen competing in the annual Striped Bass and Bluefish Derby, most of the summer boats and crowds are gone, and there's a welcome sense of space. We move slowly up the pond until Whit chooses where he wants to set the scallop drags. Idling the boat, he throws first one and then the other drag into the shallow water. Every year he forgets how heavy even the empty ones are.

We motor slowly, letting the drags run gently along the bottom. Soon they are full. Together we manage to pull up each drag and dump the contents onto the culling board. There are a few crabs, empty oyster shells, and some seaweed, but the bulk of the take is delectable bay scallops.

My favorite way to eat a scallop is raw on the boat. Before we begin the job of culling we stop and indulge in a few tender bites. Holding a scallop by its side firmly but gently, I jimmy open the crenulated shell with a scallop knife and slide the guts off to expose the sweet muscle. I scrape against the shell with a quick turn of the knife, and a perfect bite is ready to be sucked out of the shell, sweet, cold, and utterly delicious.

My second favorite way to eat bay scallops is the way my father cooked them. He added an ample chunk of butter to a cast-iron skillet and put the pan on the stove over a high flame. Watching closely to make sure the butter was hot and bubbly, but not browning, he added the scallops. When I do it, I try to make sure no scallops are touching. I like them browned on the edges, but Dad didn't care about that.

The procedure is simple, but there's skill involved. Too hot a skillet and the butter burns; not hot enough, and the scallops release their juices. Once the scallops are in the pan, Dad stirred them for a few minutes keeping the heat pretty high. When he thought they were almost ready, he poured in a generous dollop of good sherry, enough so the scallops were swimming in a butter/sherry bath. He let this simmer a minute or so to burn off some of the alcohol.

The scallops were done. All that remained was to add a little salt and pepper to taste. Sometimes Dad poured the scallops onto a bed of rice, but usually he ladled them into shallow soup bowls and we ate them with a spoon, sopping up the extra juices with a crispy slice of warm French bread.

It's hard to imagine a better setting for eating a scallop than an open boat on Menemsha pond, but Dad's den ran a close second. There was always a roaring fire. We'd settle in on overstuffed chairs, dogs at our feet, set our bowls on rickety TV tables, and dig in. The meal was so rich the only thing we could do to settle our stomachs was to follow it with a small bowl of ice cream.

Before scallop season is over this year, I hope I have the opportunity to show my two children how to cook scallops the way Dad did. Recently I learned that Dad's beloved uncle taught him this recipe. It's funny to think that when Dad and I ate scallops together we were connected in that moment, but what grounded our memories was separated by at least a generation. Will knowing this way of cooking scallops has been passed down by family members for at least a century add to my children's pleasure — or make it all too rich with meaning?

If so, we can go back to basics. Nothing beats the purity of that first raw bite — a taste the human family has enjoyed with unbridled pleasure generation after generation.

CRANBERRIES

The only place I know to see cranberries growing is in the tiny bog by the main holding pond at Cranberry Acres. A sweet trail circles this pond, and I often walk it, always pausing at the bog to see if the fruit has changed from white to a deep rich red.

Today in honor of Cranberry Day, always the second Tuesday in October, I want to go see the ripe berries. For the first time this season I take a jacket down from a peg in our mudroom and reluctantly put it on. It's cool this afternoon. Piling our two old dogs into the car, I drive the few minutes down the Lambert's Cove Road to Blackwater Pond Reservation to meet up with a friend.

We pick up the trail to Cranberry Acres alongside the Hoft Farm barn. A former road, the trail meanders through the oak and pinewoods, before ending abruptly at the main pond at Cranberry Acres. Everything is shiny in the low afternoon light. Fallen leaves hold little sparkling puddles of last night's rain. The dogs race ahead barking, delighted by the cooler weather.

The October sun glistens off the backs of turtles and the green heads of mallards dotting the pond. Following a rim of emerald green moss to the right, soon we are walking on a pair of narrow wooden boards edged on both sides by the ripe red fruit. The ground is moist and the low plants gleam. A sign posted by the Vineyard Open Land Foundation, the steward of this restoration project, reminds us to look, not pick. I want to roll a smooth skinned fruit between my fingers and rub a sprig of the tiny, shiny green leaves across my cheek. Just looking is hard, but I keep my hands in my pockets.

A peculiar abundance of animal life teems in this small pond. The ducks make a racket, and there are more turtles than we can count. Frogs create a steady stream of splashes by leaping into the water as we approach. The dappled light of the woods is cool, so when we return to the open fields of the Nature Conservancy's Hoft Farm we can't resist the pull of full sun and decide to meander through the still green fields.

At one edge, the trail skims the rim of one of the Blackwater Ponds, which I've just read were holding ponds for cranberry production. I'm describing this to Margi when we both look down. We are standing in a dense patch of cranberries. There are no signs here.

In unison we drop to the ground, kneel among the vines and begin to pick. The vine's tiny leaves are soft to the touch. Spreading them gently apart, we find fruit in abundance. Laughing with delight, I gather with both hands, grateful for the ample pockets of my warm coat. In no time they are full of luscious ripe red fruit. I keep dipping my hands into my pockets again and again to feel the smooth surface of the shiny berries slipping between my fingers. They are dry and light.

Back at my house we pool our fruits into a metal colander. There are exactly four cups, two for each of us. This is just what I need to make my favorite cranberry dessert — a cranberry walnut pie. While the oven warms I gather the ingredients and the recipe. The recipe is handwritten on the grey registration card of a bed-and-breakfast in Duluth, Iowa, where I first tasted the pie in 1998. That day it was the first course of a five-course breakfast.

It surprised me to have what I thought of as a local delicacy in Iowa. My hosts laughed at their provincial guest and told me the state of Wisconsin, just across the Mississippi River from Duluth, is the leading producer of cranberries in the United States. Massachusetts is second.

Each time I make this pie I'm amazed something so delicious can be so simple, but this time I feel a special pride because I have gathered these berries with the pleasure of my own hands. The kitchen fills with the fragrance of cooked cranberries. For a moment, I consider taking the pie to the Wampanoag potluck.

The day of harvesting cranberries from the communal bogs is for tribe members only, but the evening dancing, drumming and eating is open to everyone on the Island. It's tempting but the fire is lit, and my family will be home soon. I'm glad Cranberry Day happens every year, so tonight we can savor this unexpected autumn treat right here at home.

Cranberry Walnut Pie

9-inch unbaked pie crust
2 cups whole cranberries
1 cup whole walnut halves
$1/4$ cup brown sugar
1 egg
$1/2$ cup sugar
$1/3$ cup butter, melted and cooled
$1/2$ cup flour

Set the oven to 325 degrees. Place cranberries and walnuts in pie shell. Sprinkle with brown sugar. Combine egg, sugar, and flour. Beat well. Spread on top of fruit and nut mixture. Bake 45-50 minutes.

EMPTY NEST

Today I spotted a bird's nest in a thicket of briar on the edge of our field. Somehow it had become dislodged from the twisted vines. The nest now tipped to one side, and the soft patch at its center was crudely exposed. I could see animal hairs and downy bits of plant fluff that the parent birds had woven in to cushion first eggs, then babies. Seeing all this effort now flapping uselessly in the northeast breeze was more than I could bear. I plunged into the thicket, surprised by my urgency.

The nest was held fast by only one thorn. Detangling it was easier than I expected, and soon I was standing amid the briars, covered with scratches, holding the nest in my hand. It fit right into my palm. Both sturdy and delicate, the construction amazed me.

How does a bird know what to chose to make such a wondrous home? Nest in hand, I pulled myself back through the thicket, leaving behind a few of my own hairs on the sharp briars. Perhaps they will be used to line a new nest next season.

My husband and I just took our youngest child to Boston to start college. For the past few weeks our focus has been on packing, medical forms, course requirements, farewells. As visitors poured onto the Island for the Labor Day weekend, we quietly slipped off. Our station wagon overflowed with pillows and whatever comforts of home we could stuff into it. I noticed, gratefully, there were several other families on the boat who were doing the same thing. Their cars were also laden and their faces expressed the anticipation and sadness I felt in my own.

The next day, after a welcome speech for freshman families, a picnic in the quad, and innumerable trips up four flights of stairs into a cramped dorm room, there was nothing to do but go. Lila was launched and in a place that seemed right for her. That life could begin when we departed. She had begged us not to cry when we left so she wouldn't get upset too. We thought we had succeeded, but with the final hug came tears all around. Waving goodbye, we pulled away in our empty car and turned toward home.

The nest sits on my desk in a china saucer that belonged to my mother-in-law. It's still empty, of course, but at least it's right side up and no longer dangles in the briar patch. I hope the parents were able to lay eggs in its cavity and keep them warm. I hope chicks shed their shells here, opened their mouths for food, and gradually filled it to bursting. I hope the parents taught these babies to fly and emptied this nest before it was loosened from its mooring.

When people said, "Oh, you'll have an empty nest now!" the phrase rubbed me the wrong way, but now that I'm studying the nest beside me it makes more sense. An empty nest is clean. At home today there are no dirty dishes in the sink, no sticky negotiations for staying out late or borrowing the car. An empty nest is quiet. This weekend the TV has been blessedly off and the phone rarely rang. Although the silence is welcome, I miss the vitality and electricity that Lila stirs up.

An empty nest means the task is completed, but I'm not ready to believe my job is done. Yet Lila is off soaring solo, as she is ready to be. Last night she called from a North End festival celebrating St. Anthony and her excitement lit up the wires. She was not looking back, and I don't want her to. My briar scratches remind me that I still need to rescue a used nest, but in time I expect I'll learn better how to let go.

HOME BIRD

The departures begin as soon as the fair lights dim, even before the carnies break down the Ferris wheel. First to go are the college students and the male hummingbirds. Following them are flocks of brown cowbirds and masses of emerald-backed tree swallows, which cluster up on the rainbow-colored edge of the Gay Head cliffs in preparation for their group migration.

Many migrating birds and people grace our island through mid October, but compared to August our numbers are steadily down. Just last week the family of swans I watched all summer moved on. The three cygnets had never been more that a few paddles away from their parents, but finally first one, then another and finally the third took flight, crossing the thin strip of dune and splashing into Vineyard Sound. There are those of us who pass through, and those of us who stay.

I am one of those who stay, and, as a homebody, staying suits me. I prefer being close to home. My English cousin calls me a home bird, and it's true.

I feel a hardy kinship with those birds that come to my feeder all year long, the chickadees, the goldfinches, the cardinals. We aren't suited to continental migrations like the osprey or the ruby-throated hummingbird. When the summer season turns to autumn, instead of moving on, we hunker down.

The Island becomes quieter and more spacious again. Where leaves have fallen, views are extended and glimpses of ocean that were hidden now sparkle through. Islanders' cars fill the beach parking lots and on these Indian Summer days we can finally enjoy that summer feeling of leisure. Often the weather is mild enough for bare feet and the water still warm enough for a plunge. There can even be a final crop of tender lettuces and string beans alongside sturdy kales, chards, and squashes — if we escape a frost.

Last week this home bird found herself home alone for seven days and seven nights with no husband or children. I had always wanted this experience, but it had never happened before. I stopped by the Winter Farmer's Market at the Agricultural Hall to stock up. People shopped and ate at long trestle tables. No one seemed to be in a hurry, and the crowd was full of faces I knew once more. I bought some Good Farm chicken livers and an assortment of vegetables before heading home.

Turning off the Lambert's Cove Road into our circular drive always gives me a lift. Home again. Bright sun bounced off the red trim and added luster to our well-worn farmhouse. Striped beach towels on the line flapped a welcome wave. Pal and Derby, our two elderly black Labs, pulled themselves from under the hydrangea bushes and greeted me with ecstatic barks and wags. I might have been Odysseus returning home at last from Troy. I quickly put the food away, grabbed a light coat, and the three of us headed down into the back yard to pick up the path to Lambert's Cove Beach. It was time for a walk.

In the field next to ours I paused to admire the burnt orange leaves of a small cluster of bettlebung trees. There was movement in the upper branches. I expected to see sparrows, but these birds were dusty grey with a chest the same orange as the autumn leaves. Six of them fluttered through the trees like drops of water. One turned and veered off towards a nearby cedar tree and the sun lit up its back. The iridescent feathers were the royal blue that always opens up my heart: bluebirds! Eastern bluebirds right here, next to my own back yard. I stood and watched them dip and move until the dogs urged me down the path and over the dune to the beach.

Low tide, yet the beach was empty, even on this lovely Saturday. We walked behind a flock of small shorebirds from one end of the cove to the other. By the time we turned back for home the dogs were panting and their halting gait showed their full four-teen years. My pockets were lined with a few smooth pieces of sea glass and some round stones. I did not expect to see the bluebirds again, but there they were, in the same beetlebung trees. Now that the dogs were satisfied, I could stop and drink my fill of these beautiful songbirds. Like the swans, they were probably prepar-ing to move on, but since some pairs winter over, I pictured these bluebirds staying. Like me, perhaps they would be home birds.

The house welcomed me back and I settled in to my cozy soli-tude. What does a home bird do when she comes inside from a walk and is alone? She rests and reads until it gets dark and then she cooks.

I ate chicken livers often when I was a child and eating them reminds me of my mother. But my husband, son, and daughter do not like them. Now there was no one to please but myself. I got *The Essentials of Italian Cooking* down from the shelf and went to work.

Marcella Hazan's chicken liver sauce begins with sautéing shallots, so soon the kitchen was filled with a pungent, sweet smell. Prairie Home Companion was on the radio. Garrison Keillor can still be clever and funny after all these years. I set the kitchen table for one, poured a glass of red Chianti and lit the candles. Soon I sat down and savored first one and then another substantial and satisfying helping. My home bird week had begun.

A home bird, according to the Oxford English Dictionary, is a person who likes to stay at home, a homebody. The *American Heritage Dictionary* defines a homebody as a person who does not like to go out or travel; there is no listing for home bird. Liking to stay home is very different from not liking to go out. We home birds can enjoy going out and travelling—it's just that we find special delight in the comfort, nourishment, and complexity of our lives at home.

Marcella Hazan's Chicken Liver Sauce

4–6 SERVINGS

Best served with pappardelle noodles

1/2 pound fresh chicken livers
2 teaspoons shallot or onion
1 tablespoon vegetable oil
2 tablespoons butter
1/4 teaspoon chopped garlic very fine
3 tablespoons diced pancetta or prosciutto
4–5 whole sage leaves
1/4 pound beef chuck
salt
black pepper, ground fresh from the mill
1 teaspoon tomato paste dissolved in 1/4 cup vermouth
1 1/4 pounds homemade pasta
Freshly grated parmigiano-reggiano cheese at the table

1. Remove any greenish spots or particles of fat from the chicken livers, rinse them in cold water. Cut each liver into 3 or 4 pieces, and pat them thoroughly dry with paper towels.

2. Put the shallot or onion in a saucepan or sauté pan together with the oil and butter; turn on the heat to medium. Cook and stir the shallot or onion until it becomes translucent. Add the chopped garlic and cook it briefly, not long enough to become colored, then add the diced pancetta or prosciutto, and the sage. Stir well, cooking for about a minute or less, then add the ground beef, a large pinch of salt, and a few grindings of pepper. Crumble the meat with a fork and cook until it has lost its raw, red color.

3. Add the cut-up chicken livers, turn the heat up to medium high. Stir thoroughly and cook briefly, just until the livers have lost their raw, red color.

4. Add the tomato paste and vermouth mixture, and cook for 5 to 8 minutes, stirring from time to time. Taste and correct for salt.

5. Turn the entire contents of the pan over cooked drained pasta. Toss well, coating all the strands, and serve at once with grated Parmesan on the side.

HUMMINGBIRDS AND
OTHER VISITORS

Our back yard hummingbird feeder, a center of frantic activity in the summer months, is stowed for the winter. For weeks only a few languid wasps drank its sweet liquid. Still, I left it up in case a late-leaving hummer needed one final burst of energy for its long trip south. According to the first edition of *Vineyard Birds* by Susan Whiting and Barbara Pesch, a ruby-throated hummingbird was sited on the Island as late as October 12 in 1965. Finally, this weekend I brought the feeder inside, washed it in soapy water, wrapped each glass piece carefully in newspaper, and packed it away.

Vineyard summers are framed for me by the arrival and departure of hummingbirds. These tiny birds first appear in late April, like many of our seasonal homeowners. Often cold and exhausted from their difficult migration, these generally hyperactive birds sit on the feeder dazed and quiet for long minutes to recover their strength before drinking. Throughout the spring, ruby throats pour onto the island, initiating a frenzy of activity as nesting and mating take place and new young are born.

The only birds that can fly backwards, hummers are extraordinary aerialists and acrobats. Their behavior runs to extremes ranging from delicately sipping sugar water or nectar with long tongues to fiercely defending their turf — my feeder — with vicious lunges and loud squeaks. Their intensity is a good fit with the energy and activity that many summer visitors bring with them when they come to vacation, and want to recharge and relax and party, party, party.

As the summer wanes and the days cool and shorten, male ruby throats head back south followed a few weeks later by the females and last-hatch juveniles. Almost all depart sometime after Labor Day just when summer residents pack away their beach towels and picnic supplies and return to their real lives elsewhere. The feeder is quiet and another season has come and gone.

Summer visitors often ask, "What do you do here in the winter?" I try not to crow, but the end of the tourist season makes me buoyant. Finally we Islanders can breathe once again. Friends have time to connect, take walks or swims, and share a meal. Once again our rhythm can be our own.

Even though their departure coincides with the Island becoming more peaceful, I miss the hummingbirds when they leave. I lie awake at night and imagine their migration south, picturing them over a map of the eastern United States. What kinds of late-blooming flowers are they finding for nectar? What tiny insects are giving them the energy they need for their long trip? Are they in Georgia now, or have they already reached the great expanse of the Gulf of Mexico that they have to cross to reach their wintering grounds?

How a hummingbird, the smallest bird in North America, can fly five hundred miles over open sea non-stop for eighteen to twenty hours is a mystery to me. Somehow they manage it and settle down for the winter in the dry forests, citrus groves or scrub hedgerows of Central America. Come spring, the journey will reverse itself and the ruby throats will gradually return north to mate and build nests as far north as southern Canada — some of them, thankfully, in my yard.

I used to believe the same hummingbirds returned to my yard each season because they always perch on one particular oak branch. I've learned this is unlikely. Not unlike our human visitors, there is a July group and an August group.

In *Ruby-Throated Hummingbird,* Robert Sargent reports that hummingbirds are constantly on the move. New birds are continually coming and going. To determine how many birds you are feeding, Sargent writes, estimate the largest number at your feeder and multiply by five. I have seen as many as six at one time using my feeder. Could it be that thirty hummingbirds are making their homes nearby? How thrilling! I wish I felt as generous about the many guests that circulate through our beds during the summer months, but I don't.

It has been over six weeks since females and juveniles crowded the hummingbird feeder. These birds seemed to study me as intently as I studied them. In the final days before their departure, wherever I sat outside they would find me, flying in so close to my face that I could feel the air from their wings against my skin. Maybe this was a farewell or just a pause before we all soared into this new season.

STORM AND SKY

A strong northeast wind blew across the Island just in time for Halloween, blasting away any illusions that Indian summer might linger. The powerful wind whipped up the waves on Vineyard Sound and rattled our hundred-year-old farmhouse. Ferryboats were cancelled, snarling Vineyard Haven and bringing back our houseguest who put his dirty sheets back on the bed.

My husband and I ran from room to room dropping storm windows while our dogs took cover under our bed. Expecting to lose our electricity, we filled the claw-foot bathtub with water and gathered a hefty supply of candles, oil lanterns, and flashlights. We brought in plenty of firewood, figured out a meal we could cook on the gas burner, opened a bottle of wine, lit the fire, and settled in for a good storm. We weren't disappointed.

The wild storms that punctuate each season are part of the thrill of Vineyard life. Tomorrow when the storm has passed, the beaches will be strewn with driftwood and other treasures. Surfers will gather in the parking lots of Squibnocket and other beaches eager to challenge the huge waves. Tonight we are all home waiting it out, pacing our houses, like sea captain's wives. The whistling winds and thrashing waves accentuate our smallness, and we are grateful for neighbors whose lights, like ours, are off.

The wind reached its crescendo shortly after midnight. We lay awake in our beds listening to its howl and moan. By morning the storm had blown by, but traces of it remained everywhere. Wind and a high storm sea carved deep gullies around seaside boulders, and Lambert's Cove Beach was sharply cut. Heavy rain lingered in potholes and deep puddles. Trails in the woods were blocked by big fallen trees. Matted leaves and sticks lay atop the grass seed we'd waited too long to plant.

We are entering those months visitors question us about, wondering how we survive here when we don't have them to entertain us. It's true there is less of everything except sky and sea. Deciduous trees are stripped down. Fields have been reaped, and home gardens put to bed. Spring pigs and sheep have been slaughtered. There are fewer homes lit at night and when I'm driving up Island in the evening I can often count on one hand the number of cars I see.

Daylight savings begins this Sunday and falling back is hard. The afternoons are over so quickly. Whit checks the Farmer's Almanac each day and calls out the number of minutes lost until winter solstice, when the days start getting longer little by little once again. This season I'm noticing that with less comes more: more sky, more moon watching, more time to see friends, to read, to cook, to walk. I am enjoying the paring down. I look forward to the hard frost that will sweeten the carrots and provide a clean break to a new season.

There is something benign about lying in the grass in August and watching the predictable parade of shooting stars from the Perseid meteor shower. This is a soft kind of wonder. The huge winter sky is altogether different. With Orion in ascendance, the sky opens wider and wider as leaves fall and naked branches reveal yet more constellations, more universes, a multitude of suns.

I dress warmly, wear boots and gloves and challenge myself to really study the sharp night sky. Almost immediately its vastness overwhelms me. I love our watery planet so fiercely that I have to look away. Any thoughts about our significance falter. Thank goodness for the moon, our close companion. It's comforting to know that no matter where we are we are all looking at the same moon.

Now that I've lived on the Island for many years, I find these stripped down months are what keep me here. The short days hone something essential inside me. The long nights, swirling with galaxies I can't comprehend, challenge me and whet my appetite for spare simple truths. When all the fanfare falls away, I remember again how sturdy my love is for my family, for people and animals, for plants and stones and all the blessings of this earth.

WINTER

A WINTER WALK

Finally, I was alone at my desk, ready to write. Yet just a single nudge from a soft black muzzle, and I was in the mudroom pulling on my jacket, fumbling for a hat, ready to go. After yesterday's rain and relentless grey, the world seemed washed to glistening, the need to step out urgent.

I watched myself get the dogs into the car, adjust the seat, turn on the ignition, amazed. How had I abandoned my work without any apparent struggle? Hadn't I fought hard for the privilege of sitting in that chair? Was it reading William Faulkner with my morning tea? In a single sentence of *Pantaloon in Black*, he said more about love and grief and time and race and humanity than seemed possible. No wonder my page remained blank.

I didn't think I had a plan, but the car turned up Island at the end of Lambert's Cove Road, veered southwest past Alley's into Chilmark and turned in at the Quansoo Road. This was no longer the dusty slow road of August lined with the big cars of impatient beach key holders. Now the gate leans open, gesturing a wide welcome for us winter folk. My tire tracks are the first since last night's rain swept the dirt clear. A twist, a turn, a bump or two, and then just sand, shrub, water and sky, sky, sky.

This dormant time is why I live here. This pause when one season is behind and the preparations for the next have yet to begin. Now Islanders can fully explore, not the unknown, but the familiar we forget to pay attention to. I park among puddles. The dogs pop out, tails up. There is the footbridge, the creek, and the sandy path slipping up and over the dune. Are there words to describe the sun on Black Point Pond? For a moment I try to grab for the names of colors, tones, feelings and then leave it for someone else. Faulkner would know, but for me it is enough to stand here saturated by its glory.

The turbulent surf and huge waves surprise me as I crest the dune. The hills of sand had muffled the ocean's ferocity. The beach, like the road, is wiped clean by yesterday's weather. Ours are the first tracks belonging to human or dog. I pretend I'm Robinson Crusoe as I mosey along picking up pieces of peat, a pair of crab claws, and a few white feathers. There's a swirl of shells dumped so exquisitely that I wonder, is there a better artist than the sea itself?

By the time we turn back, pushed by sand and wind, I'm singing as loudly as I can an old ballad about stalking the shore. "Dear wind that blows the body free, blow home my true love's ship to me. Fill his sails." Too quickly we're back in the parking lot where our car waits alone. The wet dogs climb in the back, my treasures go between the seats, and I'm ready for an egg salad sandwich—and even the blank sheet of paper on my desk.

HUNTING DUCKS

Bird hunting, with all its rituals and rites, was at the center of our family life on the eastern end of Long Island. It absorbed my father like nothing else. From dawn on opening day in late November until the last January afternoon of the season, Dad hunted the brackish ponds and turned-under potato fields morning and evening for goose, duck, pheasant, and woodcock.

Duck hunting was Dad's favorite and sometimes I was invited to go along. Those mornings Dad shook me awake in the pitch dark and we drove forty-five minutes to Hampton Bays in silence. The walk in our heavy boots to the blind at the Head of the Creek was precarious in places on sagging boards, but once I settled in on the wooden bench between my father and Shell, our quivering springer spaniel, I felt elated. We shared a thermos of black coffee and I always burned my tongue. As the morning light seeped into the marsh, all three of us scanned the purple sky for ducks.

On one of these trips, when I was nine or ten, I fired a shotgun for the first time. Dad had shown me how to aim his uncle's .410 at a scrub oak and pretend to pull back the trigger, but that morning he told me to take off the safety and shoot. I did. The unexpected violence of the recoil jammed my shoulder, and I almost dropped the precious gun. Tears ran down my cheeks. I didn't want Dad to think I was soft, but the truth was, I didn't want to wound or kill anything, not even a tree.

During the hunting season, dinners waited until we heard Dad's honk and Shell's excited bark. They were home! Any birds bagged that day were carefully spread out in the back of the station wagon. Teal, mallards, and the occasional canvasback were admired, then carried by their necks to the kitchen porch where they were hung on nails by their beaks to season for a few days. Next the gear was tended to. Decoys were put away or readied for the morning and all guns were broken down, cleaned and put back in the gun case.

Dad usually hunted with a 16-gauge Hammerlock that he "liberated" during the war, or a Belgian 12-gauge Francotte. By the time I was seven, I was adept at cleaning the insides of a barrel, applying the sweet-smelling oil, and wiping the wooden stocks with a soft chamois cloth. I never fired a shotgun again, but I earned the nickname Laura Sharp Eyes and a place in the blind because I often heard the whistle of wings or spotted a pair coming our way before any of my companions did.

The landscape of eastern Long Island and the men who hunted and fished it are imprinted deep inside me. The first time I visited Martha's Vineyard in the winter, I found myself in a cold blind on Tisbury Great Pond, waiting for the sun to rise. I felt right at home. The shivering dog beside me was now a yellow Labrador retriever, and the man I leaned against would become my husband. Mornings and evenings found us in Philip Spaulding's blind at the end of Tiah's Cove. Geoff Muldaur often came, too. Instead of sharing a thermos of black coffee, we opened and ate oysters we had raked up, waiting for a flight of ducks to notice our decoys, set their wings and drop in.

Frequently we came home empty handed, but sometimes we held the soft neck feathers of a black duck or a mallard. We'd breast the birds and quickly sauté the lean burgundy meat in butter. I'd serve them with the currant mustard sauce my mother made, a taste from childhood that recaptured the magic of those early dawns.

That taste will never fail to thrill me. But during the 1980s, as our lives turned to having and raising children, our attitudes began to shift. While Whit and I still loved to eat the wild meat, there was no longer any thrill in killing an animal as it eased into a pond for shelter, calling out to other birds. One evening as he squatted in the dunes near our house on James Pond in West Tisbury, staring up at the new moon, Whit realized he didn't need to carry a gun to watch the sunset. He walked home, cleaned his gun, and hasn't used it since. Even Dad, who hunted up through his seventies, gradually lost his lust for the kill. He claimed it was because there were fewer birds and his eyes were going, but I'm not sure that was it.

What I notice is I am more and more attached to the living beauty of wild things, especially birds. Now when I hear shots from the pond shore below our house, I'm rooting for the ducks, hoping the hunters have missed their mark. While Shell quivered with excitement for the hunt, Pal, our current dog, a black lab/golden mix, is terrified by the sound of gunfire. When hunters open fire she cowers under our bed shaking with fear.

I miss the smell of gun oil and the intimacy of those dark expectant mornings. But I'll still trade the sharp scent of a clean kill, even with its promise of a succulent dinner, for the whistling of black ducks' wings as they land undisturbed on the neighboring field in the cold, still night.

NORTHERN ORIOLE

One Sunday morning in early January there was a fluffy orange mound huddled in the tray of my birdfeeder. It looked an awful lot like a Baltimore oriole, but this seemed impossible. I flipped through the pages of the *Sibley Guide to Birds*, hoping the bird belonged to another species, one more suited to surviving our winters. Most likely, though, I had seen a juvenile male northern oriole, as Baltimores are now called. The rest of the morning I kept one eye on the Sunday crossword puzzle and the other on the feeder, but he did not return.

I grew up in Washington, D.C., and know only too well the differences between those mild winters and the stinging bitter cold we can have here on the Island. This week it felt like the cold would never loosen its iron grip. Temperatures stayed below freezing. My breath hung in the frigid air. Each morning the water in the birdbath was frozen and each morning I replaced the block of ice. Over the next few days I spent a surprising amount of time wondering and worrying about this beautiful bird. Was he hungry, cold? Could he survive our sharp winter?

Whenever I was home, I hovered by the windows near the birdfeeder, finding reasons to fold laundry or cook or pay bills in close proximity. But there was never any sign of him. Maybe he had moved on. Northern orioles, like most of our summer visitors, usually pass through the Island from May to September. Some nest here, but most move on. Winter sightings, though not unprecedented, are unusual. Northern orioles should be wintering in Mexico or the Caribbean or even as far south as the northern part of South America, not shivering in snowy, windswept West Tisbury.

Two mornings later the bird was back, sitting in the feeder tray with his feathers fluffed out, picking at a sunflower seed. This time I had the presence of mind to grab a digital camera and take some photographs. I got Soo Whiting, friend and bird expert, on the phone and she asked some key questions. What colors were the wings? They were black and white. What part of it was orange? Almost all.

I emailed her a selection of photos and she immediately responded, "Go to the head of the class! Yes indeed, you have a Baltimore oriole at your feeder! I will report it to Rob Culbert as this is still during count period of the Christmas Bird Count, and I don't think anyone else spotted an oriole. Thanks so much."

At first I was pleased to have identified the bird correctly and that the sighting would contribute to the bird count. But then I started to worry: if no one else had spotted an oriole, was this bird the only one here?

"What are his chances for making it?" I wrote back to Soo.

Her answer was not encouraging. "It will be tough for this bird to survive. I might try putting out a halved orange and maybe some jelly. They will need sugar. Not sure if the orange or jelly will survive the cold, but during the sunshine they may warm up enough so the bird can feed a bit."

I immediately went out and bought some oranges. On a walk with my neighbor Debby Farber of Blackwater Farm I told her about the bird and she went home and nailed an orange to a tree in her yard. An oriole's typical diet includes nectar, along with caterpillars, insects, and spiders. This bird would not find much in the wild to sustain him right now.

I pictured this lovely bird lingering, like so many of us, seduced by our warm November days. Was he reluctant to leave the charms of the Island, or had someone been feeding him fruit or suet? Someone who now had returned to a city or retreated farther south himself for the winter. These thoughts made me angry. The orange half sat untouched on my feeder tray for days. I kept replacing it in case the oriole returned, and I made sure the water bowl was fresh and the feeder filled. I wanted this bird to make it with a raw urgency. I knew it was irrational to tie my own winter survival to this bird, but our well-being had become intertwined.

A few days later, my daughter left me a note near my computer. "Mom, Debby called. The oriole is at her house now." It's a short flight from my yard to her farm. In just a few wing beats he could cross a field with a small pond, pass her barn and cow pasture and be in her cozy yard. I was elated.

Debby and I exchange information daily about our oriole. We discuss whether or not he's been sighted, what he's eating and whether or not he seems cold. I often stop by her house in the hopes of seeing him. At the moment we're keeping our fingers crossed and the oranges fresh. The days are getting slightly longer and the sun is packing a bit more punch. Right now, hope runs high.

POND SKATING

When I got back this morning from a walk there was a message waiting from my husband: "Skating on Parsonage." Shallow and protected, Parsonage Pond in West Tisbury is one of the first ponds to freeze over. I grabbed my skates and drove over.

Already cars and trucks lined the road, and people of all ages were sitting by the fence pulling on heavy socks and lacing up skates. Two teenaged boys were on the ice. Soon a young mother was pulling a sled with her bundled baby in it and small children in new skates or boots leaned on milk crates to help find their footing. A few dogs squeezed out of truck windows and added to the fun by barking, racing, and sliding around the edges.

A tentative skater, I wobble and my ankles buckle. Even with extra socks my skates are too big. I have a healthy fear of ice, but can't resist the romance of sliding on top of a frozen world. Besides, I love to watch my husband skate. Whit fully inhabits his body on skates, moving with grace and exuberance as he leans first one way and then the other. Watching him at Parsonage Pond today, I was reminded of the time he fell in here years ago carrying our infant daughter. As he stood waist deep in the shallow water, he slid Lila across the ice to some young boys who grabbed her by the parka hood and skated as fast as they could to where I waited on the shore, stunned.

I returned to Parsonage Pond for a second skate in the afternoon. Hockey players appeared and teams quickly formed up. In the waning light, the clack of sticks and the sharp scratch of skate blades reverberated in the crisp air. Pleasure skaters arrived with hot chocolate and warm cookies, but the hockey players weren't tempted. No one wanted to stop, and they played into the dark using headlights to illuminate the pond.

We all knew this day of skating was a precious gift, maybe one of only two or three this winter. The forecast calls for continued cold, which is hopeful, but it may snow on Monday when the moon will be full – the Snow Moon.

The hope is that this will be one of those winters when the cold days string together, and even the bigger ponds freeze, and for a short, wondrous time skating will become an everyday thing. When this happens skates and socks and sticks are kept at the ready in trucks and cars. Lunch hours are stretched and afternoon hours are shortened. The hockey players are always at it. The more ardent among them, like my son, Sam, work hard to keep a good playing surface and can be spotted flooding the surface of Duarte's Pond at night or scraping the surface of Uncle Seth's Pond with shovels and brooms. Sam lives in New York now, but he will already have heard about the promise of pond hockey and, with luck, he'll be able to come home for a couple of days to enjoy it.

Most epic, and rarest, are those times when Squibnocket Pond freezes solid. We head up Island no matter how windy and cold it is. Stories are shared of former winters, even as new memories are laid down in scratches across the ice. Skaters pour onto the ice and iceboats, usually stored away, skim across the surface. The last time this happened I joined a pod of skaters and we tacked and beat our way towards Gay Head against the northwest wind until we couldn't go any farther. Then we turned, spread out our arms, and let the wind blow us back.

Tonight I'm stiff in places I'd forgotten I even had, but I feel great. Bouncing over rough spots and sailing along on the wind offer a freedom and delight no indoor rink can simulate. Cold face, cold hands, and cold feet are well worth it when you can glide along under a flight of swans and hear the roar of the ocean surf just across the dunes — alone but with the welcome proximity of neighbors and friends skating nearby.

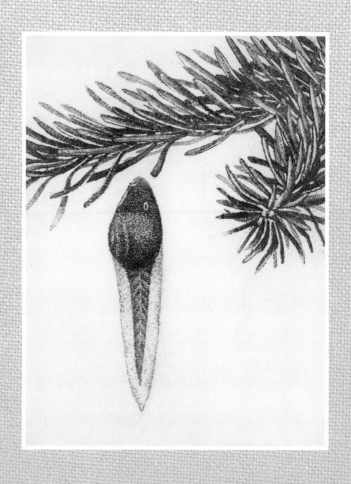

SEA GLASS

When the northeast wind blows the winter beach smooth and wipes the sand clean of footprints, I call my friend Gina and invite her to go beachcombing at Lambert's Cove Beach. We walk along the shore, our eyes fixed on the high tide line. Amid the bits of shell, seaweed, and driftwood there just might be a few pieces of sea glass.

Bundled up in parkas, scarves, and boots, we still can't avoid the damp cold that seeps into our fingers and toes. Too quickly the afternoon bleeds into a purple evening and we need a sign, an omen, some bright piece of color. Usually we find a few small pieces and pass them back and forth to admire their color and wonder about their salty history. Any jagged pieces we toss back into the sea to weather some more, but we slip the smooth pieces into our pockets or mittens so we can rub them between our fingers.

Old-timers like my neighbor Cary Luckey easily filled their pockets with sea glass when they walked the Cove in the fifties. With little plastic and no recycling, sea glass was being manufactured all the time then. But times have changed, and now it is a dwindling treasure.

I've collected sea glass since I was a child. Small bowls filled with sea glass rest on windowsills and tables throughout our house. A huge mason jar on top of the bookcase in our study holds the largest pieces. It is almost full. I've always appreciated the shape, color, and feel of sea glass. Although I've known that it can take twenty years for a piece of sea glass to weather, I've never given much thought to where the glass came from, what it was used for, or how old it might be.

A friend who knew of my interest in sea glass gave me a copy of *Pure Sea Glass: Discovering Nature's Vanishing Gems* by Richard LaMotte. Organized by color, the book gives the composition and history of many kinds of glass. Now I am acutely aware that each piece of sea glass is a nugget of history, and by matching the color and shape to the book, I can uncover that story.

This afternoon Gina and I filled our pockets with heart rocks, but we also found three small pieces of sea glass. When we came inside from our cold walk, I lit the fire and made us hot cups of peppermint tea. After we warmed up, I got out the book and we compared our little pieces to the book's lovely pictures.

The Kelly green chunk was probably part of a Coke bottle made in the 1950s, possibly even bottled at the old Coca-Cola Plant in Vineyard Haven. Our cobalt blue piece likely started as a medicine bottle manufactured in the late 1800s. The tiny pale lime green chip that Gina found near Coca-Cola Brook is a green I've never seen before. Too thin to have come from a soda bottle, we learn this color is uncommon. Found only once for every fifty pieces of glass, the pieces are usually shards, small and rounded. According to the author, it was probably made in the mid to late 1900s.

After Gina leaves, I decide to sort my whole collection of sea glass by color, according to the author's rarity scale. I could never do this in the frenzy of summer, but the short winter days make space for this.

I place four sheets of white copier paper on the dining room table and label each one: Extremely Rare, Rare, Uncommon, and Common. The wind rattles the storm windows, so I add more wood to the fire and put on a Mozart piano concerto before gathering up my stashes of sea glass and pouring them into a large salad bowl. I begin sorting. There are many colors I don't have, like orange and yellow, but the range I do have, including a few nuggets of red found on the island of Vieques, surprises me.

My daughter Lila joins me. We hold each piece of glass up to a light, compare it to the photographs in the book and try to decide which pile it should go in. We look back at the book, read the history, and then reexamine the glass, savoring its beauty. It is late when we finally finish, leaving a sea glass pie, organized by colors, in the center of the table.

Lila looks over my shoulder to the display of old bottles on the dining room windowsill. This is another collection I've created over the years with bottles harvested from Island beaches and various bottle dumps in our back yard. Tomorrow I'll delve into the chapters on bottle history and identification, but for today I am satisfied. Sunrise is early tomorrow and I want to be up.

Grading Rarity Based on Color

Extremely Rare: Orange, Red, Turquoise, Yellow, Black, Teal, Gray

Rare: Pink, Aqua, Cornflower Blue, Cobalt Blue, Opaque White, Citron, Purple/Amethyst

Uncommon: Soft Green, Soft Blue, Forest Green, Lime Green, Golden Amber, Amber, Jade

Common: Kelly Green, Brown, White (Clear)

WINTER IN THE BARN

The shortest days have come and gone. The holidays, with their open houses and potluck suppers up and down the Island, are over. The frenzy of shopping has stopped. We rang in the New Year with kisses at midnight and toasts of champagne. Daylight hours show little sign of lengthening, so we are grateful for those outdoor lights that remain up. Winter is truly upon us, and the Island has moved into its quietest months.

Island winters are demanding for even the hardiest among us. Last night the thermometer dropped into the teens, and there was no wind to keep ice from forming on the ponds. Although I heard geese working hard to keep a patch of James Pond open, the water was frozen solid this morning. Sea smoke hung over Vineyard Sound, hiding a huge raft of eider ducks. Their lovely black and white feathers dapple the beaches along the north shore and when I walk there, I collect them with thickly mittened hands.

We drive the dark away with book groups, knitting clubs, and other social activities. People meet at the gym, at Alley's Store for coffee, or make dates for walks. I find what particularly grounds me during these cold, short days are animals, especially cows. When I lean into the sturdiness of their big flanks and feel the warmth of their breath, I am fortified. The tender way they lick their lanky calves always makes me smile.

Blackwater Farm is right across the road from my house. This time of year, I often walk over at afternoon feeding time. Even before I enter the barn, I hear the clink of stanchions, slurp of water, and munching of grain. Farmers Debby and Alan are chatting as they work. Their two dogs, Cheddar and Sugar, greet me with jubilant barks and wags. Two new calico kittens dart by hoping for a pat.

The barn smells of manure and hay, horses and cows. Chickens wander through, clucking and cawing. The two big draft horses, Jack and Ruby, are deep in their grain buckets. I run my hands through Jack's thick coat, and he flicks his tail at me. There are four solid cows, each still nursing a summer calf. The mothers are fed in the stanchions while their babies feed in the box stall, which makes for a lot of mooing back and forth.

I always approach Swanlee first. Her patient white face is blotched with black freckles. I take off my mittens and offer her stale bread from my pocket. She licks me with her warm, wet tongue, and I rub my face against her sturdy neck. We've known one another for fourteen years.

Swanlee is an old lady now. She has given birth to fifteen babies. Buttercup, the baby Swanlee is nursing, will be her last. The other calves must sense Swanlee's lack of energy. They nurse off her udder, and she no longer pushes or kicks them away, like the other mothers do.

Once I feed Swanlee, I help with the farm chores. There are eggs to collect, buckets of water to fill, food to dispense. The cows and horses need go back out into the field. The chickens need to be shut in. The cats need food. The work is immediate, twice daily, relentless, and real.

This afternoon as I gather eggs and watch the calves languidly nursing in the dimming field, I decide to make eggnog. Usually this is something I make during the holidays, but not this year. There were too many gifts to make and wrap, too many visitors and parties. Now there is time and no less need for cheer.

I fill three cartons with eggs and pile them in my arms. It's satisfying to know the egg yolks will be from these familiar chickens and the cream from a cow like Swanlee. The eggnog will need time to season for four or five days, but there's no rush. Giving Swanlee's nose a final rub and promising to bring Debby and Alan some eggnog when it's ready, I head for home.

Solitude Farm Eggnog
MAKES ONE GALLON – 16–20 SERVINGS

18 eggs
1¹/₄ cups sugar
3 cups brandy (Coronet VSP)
2 cups rum (Old Mr. Boston dark)
2 quarts half and half
Nutmeg

Using a hand-held mixer at high speed, beat the egg yolks until they are pale yellow (save the whites to make meringues). Continuing to beat at high speed, add the sugar, one spoonful at a time. The mixture will be pale and creamy. In the same way, add the liquor, one tablespoon at a time. Divide this mixture into two large bowls and add a quart of half and half to each one. Blend very well. Store the eggnog in a gallon container in the refrigerator for four to five days before serving. Serve cold. Top each cup with a little freshly grated nutmeg.

SPRING

ESTATE SALE

I run through the tall grass to Cary's house next door to get a number from the auctioneer. The path has not been used in a while. By the time I get to her kitchen door, dew soaks the cuffs of my jeans. The lilac against the house has hardly any flowers. No one has tended it since Cary died three years ago at ninety-five. In two weeks her house will be sold.

Bare feet from the same two families have worn down the grass path connecting her house and mine for seventy-five years. Four generations have shared days that began with a morning swim and ended with a communal dinner under star-filled skies.

The connection began during the Depression. In 1937 my in-laws, Whit and Mary Griswold, bought the house we now live in. They were looking for a quiet summer retreat and found it here overlooking James Pond in West Tisbury. Cary and her husband, Bob Luckey, purchased the land next door a year later. There was no house on it, so they bought an old Cape from the Hough family up in Indian Hill, and had it flaked and moved by truck to Lambert's Cove.

Eventually these two summer houses became year-round homes, and the path was used during the off-season too. Cary moved back to her house full-time after the death of her second husband and lived alone with her dog, Tiga Pie. We moved into the family home for a year's experiment of living on the Island full-time and never left.

Cary and I would meet often for a sandwich or an evening drink. We'd toast the winter quiet and look forward to the raucous summers when her son and his family arrived from New Haven. Before going to bed each night I'd look out our bathroom window to make sure Cary's front door light was lit.

By 8:45 a.m., the field next door is full of cars. A line of people waits on Cary's back porch. Many seem to be estate sale regulars. They've arrived with shopping bags and warm cups of coffee, and they greet one another casually. The familiar screech of the aluminum storm door announces the sale has begun and the first twenty of us are ushered in through the living room door. It feels odd walking into Cary's living room with a group of strangers. The sight of her faded pink couch is comforting, but it has been moved to a new position and there is a price tag on it.

It is important to me to be here, but I have no idea what I am looking for. Maybe it is just to stand in these rooms one last time. Knickknacks crowd tables and most things look worn. People come in quickly and choose things in a hurry. I pick up an Indian basket, an old kerosene lamp, and a faded hooked rug mainly because I don't know what to do with my hands.

I go into each room. The quilt on the upstairs bed is one of ours. Carried over one night for a sleepover, it remained. In the guesthouse is a pile of DVDs, and several belong to my daughter. There is more than one book with my name on the inside cover — summer trades. Overwhelmed by memories, I step into the yard and there are our old Labs lying under the lilac as they often used to do.

I carry the basket, lamp, and rug along the path to home feeling empty-handed. I show them to my husband and he decides to have one last look, too. Twenty minutes later, he walks back across our yard carrying the chair Cary sat in at her kitchen table and seven cheap champagne glasses. When I put them in the dishwasher that evening I remember that I'd bought the glasses years ago as a birthday present for Cary's daughter-in-law Ettie, a dear friend. There were eight then. Finally I'm laughing. Do I really imagine an object can contain those precious years of living side by side? They have vanished like the eighth glass. I can't wait to call Ettie and tell her the story.

A few weeks later an orange-yellow half moon is setting over James Pond as I walk into Cary's yard. The grass is uncut and the peonies have not been picked. I peek in the window and see the house is utterly empty. No one is here but the three deer I startle, grazing by the pond shore, and a skunk rooting right where the new owners plan to put in a pool. No one will know if I sit here on the deck and watch the moon, but this house belongs to someone new now, and I'm trespassing. I turn on the unclipped path and head back home. Before going to bed, I catch myself looking out the bathroom window for the front door light next door. For now, it remains off.

GUILTY PLEASURE

The clear call of a goldfinch draws me back to the feeder hanging over the old lilac bush by our kitchen porch. Just days ago he was a dusty yellow, shaking off his winter coat of olive green. Now, despite the wind and the cold, he is as bright as the forsythia and those few brave daffodils daring to open in the yard. I pause, pull a chair next to the glass storm door, and settle into a pool of sun. For the next few minutes, I'll enjoy the pleasure of watching the birds come and go.

Birds aren't the only animals drawn to the sunflower seeds I put out each morning. Squirrels are adept at stealing a meal when they can, and I've learned that rats are snugly burrowed in the roots of our lilac under a thick layer of fallen seed. Skunks enjoy feeding on the seed and they especially like eating baby rats. This is where our problems began.

One rainy March night, we came home after a delicious dinner with friends to an overwhelming odor of skunk. We suspected that our two old dogs had been sprayed, but they smelled fine. The stink, oddly, was seeping up from the basement through a heating vent. I stamped my foot on the wooden floor next to the vent. This resulted in a new tangy barrage of stink and an outpouring of squealing. Not only did we have a number of skunks, they were holding their ground. The next morning we borrowed a Have-a-Heart trap, baited it with peanut butter crackers, and set it in the middle of the basement.

No luck. We'd wake up with our eyes stinging, but the peanut butter cracker in the trap remained untouched and the trap was empty. Tempers flared. The laundry piled up because no one wanted to go down to the basement and wash it. The skunks were clearly bolder than we were. Finally we wised up and called the skunk catcher.

When he saw the full bird feeder so close to the house, the skunk catcher shook his head. He pointed out the established rat colony it supported. His trained eye quickly identified many well-worn skunk paths in our yard and several places where they entered and exited the basement. While he set up his arsenal of traps, I slipped inside and hid the thirty-pound bag of sunflower seeds I'd just bought in the front hall closet. There was no reason to draw attention to it. I knew who was responsible for our problem.

For the next week or so, the skunk catcher came each morning early and reset the traps each evening. Gradually the spraying and squabbling diminished, and finally it ceased. By the time he took the last trap away, he'd captured ten skunks. The basement was empty. At last the piles of laundry could be done and the holes could be plugged to prevent the skunks from coming back. Our son, Sam, and his friend, Danny Merry, scrunched into the crawl spaces and filled each hole with cement. It was messy, difficult work, and it took two full days. Add it all up, and my guilty pleasure had turned into a very expensive treat, a luxury really. I don't think we'll be taking a vacation this year.

LADY'S SLIPPERS

Debby Farber and I, eager as any mushroom hunters, tramp the moist May paths of Duarte's Pond, Waskosim's Rock, Cranberry Acres, and Sepiessa on the lookout for lady's slippers. First come the two leaves thrusting through the damp spring soil, followed quickly by the single stem and finally the blossom that swells and deepens to a bright pink.

By mid-May these wild orchids poke into the dappled sunlight of woodland paths overshadowed by oaks and beeches. Peeking out from under low green shrubbery, they are a vision on the brown leaf-strewn forest floor. No wonder Native American lore has it that the lady's slipper can be used to induce spirit dreams.

At an early age I was taught never to pick nor in any way disturb a lady's slipper. It was a good lesson. The lady's slipper, also known as the moccasin flower, is a protected species that only grows under special circumstances.

Most plants develop seeds that contain their own food supply and nutrients, but the seeds of a lady's slipper do not. Instead, they rely on the presence of a particular fungus in the soil whose threads break open the seeds and provide necessary food and nutrients. It's a symbiotic relationship, but the fungus has to wait a long time for its reward. A new lady's slipper plant can take years to develop, but when it finally matures, its roots will return the favor to the fungus by providing it with essential nutrients.

An established lady's slipper can live for twenty years or more if left alone. Debby and I have been watching for the flowers long enough to know where many will come up. We greet them like old friends back after a long journey. In one spot, we can expect to see as many as seventy flowers, but I won't say where that is.

Once a lady's slipper is mature enough to bloom it needs the help of another creature — the bee. Attracted by the sweet smell, a bee will enter the closed flower. Once inside, it becomes trapped. To get out, the bee must climb to the neck of the flower and squeeze through the small opening. As it does, the bee brushes its back against the stamens and exits the lady's slipper flower covered with pollen. Usually, the bee can't resist diving into another pink blossom, and pollination takes place. Debby and I often sit on the damp ground and watch bees push against the fleshy blossoms in their struggle to get out.

It's humbling how many specific factors must align for each small lady's slipper plant to become established, mature, and finally bloom. So much in our culture is available instantly now that it's hard to imagine the patience of a fungus that waits years to be repaid for helping a lady's slipper seed get its start. What faith!

And what a delicate balance. No wonder Debby and I are both reassured and comforted when we see these lovely flowers coming up once again in their rightful place, spring after spring.

PAINTED TURTLES

Chores push our walk at Duarte's Pond into the evening. By that time the water lilies are tightly closed and there are no painted turtles on the log where they usually bask in the hot part of the day. Two friends and I pause on the wooden causeway to watch the swallows dip and soar, skimming the still surface of the pond for insects. We could linger longer, but our dogs urge us on.

Walking silently amid wild laurel and fragrant black locust, I try to figure out what it is about the sight of a painted turtle that fills me with happiness. Is it the funny way they maneuver into the water, so still and then so quick? The satisfying plop when they hit the water? Or is it simply the thrill of a moment's connection with such an ancient animal?

Turtles have been making their homes on our planet for more than two hundred million years. Once, they lived side by side with dinosaurs. They watched the arrival of mammals and witnessed the gradual emergence of human beings. Safe in their armored shells, they endured and adapted to every manner of change in climate and geology.

The early evening glow glazes the woods in soft amber light. After meandering through my favorite beech grove, we emerge into an open field and stumble onto an abundance of wild strawberries. Kneeling in the damp grass, we graze on the tiny fruit, staining our fingers a satisfying rich red. It's time to pick up the pieces of our daily lives, but we stall, reluctant to give up this moment.

When we move on, our pace is faster. It's getting to be dinnertime. That's when we notice the painted turtle on the edge of the sandy road. Straddling a conical hole about three inches deep, it is hard at work. It ducks its head into its shell for a few moments but soon eases back out, apparently unfazed by the presence of three middle-aged women and four dogs. Any thoughts of leaving evaporate. We shoo away the dogs and settle down to watch.

A glimpse of white by the tail emerges and transforms into an ovoid gelatinous egg. The size of a small grape, it drops soundlessly into the nest. Our turtle is a she. With her back left foot, the mother pats the egg gently into place. After a pause of a minute, maybe two, the process begins again.

The nest's position is horribly vulnerable. A car approaches, and we signal the driver to stop so we can point out the turtle and her nest. We mark the place with sticks so people will avoid it when they pass by. The driver says she'll be careful and alert the others who live along the road, but her passenger tells us this happened last spring too, and the eggs did not survive.

The turtle continues her work. She deposits four more eggs into her nest as we watch, crouching next to her in the twilight. I notice she uses the same back leg to position the egg the way she wants it: she's a lefty like me.

None of us want to move, but finally we leave her. Unable to stay away, I return half an hour later with my son. The nest has been smoothed over and the turtle has disappeared. The sticks we positioned nearby are the only signs anything happened here. Her job is done. With luck these eggs will hatch in seventy-two to eighty days and the babies will make their way to the water on their own; easy prey for a hungry predator. We want these eggs to make it. I mark off the hatch dates on my calendar and picture myself shepherding tiny turtle babies down the hill and into the pond.

The next morning I check the nest again. It has been savaged. The ground is dug up and bits of shell, now hardened, are strewn around. My spirit sinks. Had we somehow alerted a predator to the nest's presence?

How any turtle survives seems miraculous. Each step from egg to maturity is fraught with danger. Raccoons, skunks, snakes, hawks, snapping turtles, dogs, ants, deer and human beings top the long list of possible predators. It's discouraging but not surprising to learn that turtles are threatened worldwide.

Imagine being wired with everything you need to know from the moment you are born. So much about being human involves instruction and practice. Rain or shine my mother insisted I go outside and stay outside. I spent a lot of time poking into holes with sticks, wandering in the mud of our pond, and testing how far I dared venture before I got scared. This forced exploration was one of the best gifts Mom gave me. Now, years later, I can count on the natural world to ground me and reset my sense of what truly matters.

It's a comfort to learn that sometimes a painted turtle lays two clutches. Already there may be a new batch of eggs waiting to hatch.

BLUEBIRDS THRILL ME

Bluebirds thrill me. Every time I catch a glimpse of a royal blue back or the smudge of a rusty breast, a rush of happiness pours through me. Most bluebirds are seasonal visitors to the Island, stopping here from early spring to late fall, but some pairs choose to stay.

A few of these lovely songbirds wintered over this year near the John Hoft Farm off Lambert's Cove Road. In early March they started congregating near the fence around the farm's Native Plant Nursery. On the afternoons when I was free, I'd stand quietly by the fence and watch them drop to the ground from the fence posts, snatch up insects, and rise back up to their perches. The late afternoon light illuminating their backs sustained my belief in spring.

A dozen homemade bluebird boxes circle the fence, and I examined them daily for signs of use. Although bluebirds naturally nest in tree cavities or old woodpecker holes, they have adapted comfortably to nesting boxes. One afternoon, I saw a female bluebird emerge from a nest box with a piece of grass held delicately in her beak; I hoped she was making a nest.

Bluebirds were common when settlers cleared forests to create fields and orchards. Severe winter weather, changes in the landscape, pesticides, and the careless introduction of house sparrows and starlings from England drastically reduced their numbers by the middle of the twentieth century. Bluebird populations reached their lowest ebb in 1963. The only bluebird I saw growing up was on a postage stamp.

What was true nationwide was also true here on the Island: by the early 1980s, bluebirds were uncommon. In the first edition of *Vineyard Birds*, published in 1983, Susan B. Whiting and Barbara Pesch reported, "Sadly, this lively species has declined dramatically in the past two decades. Formerly a locally common summer resident, at present only a few pairs nest on the Island."

Some afternoons when I visited the Hoft Farm, bluebird song was the only evidence that the birds were nearby. Their song is a languid warble with a mellow, liquid quality that I find sensuous and moving. It's terrible to think this voice was almost lost.

In *Silent Spring*, published in 1962, Rachel Carson deplored the absence of birdsong. Her words galvanized the environmental movement. DDT was banned in 1972. Bluebirds were helped by the establishment of bluebird trails. Volunteers set up bluebird boxes and monitored them regularly. When they found a nest in a bluebird box that belonged to another species, they removed it. This work, which continues today, has paid off. In 1987, bluebirds were removed from the federal government's list of Species of Special Concern.

Bluebird populations have also recovered here on the Island. In *Vineyard Birds II*, published in 2007, Whiting and Pesch describe the bluebird as a "common summer resident and transient. Formerly uncommon, it is now a resident and breeder on the Island. This is undoubtedly due in part to an increase of bluebird boxes put up in the last twenty-four years."

Throughout March and early April I returned to the Hoft Farm hoping for a lift, and I often got it. Whenever I saw a bluebird I came home softer on my feet and brighter in spirit. Lately my efforts have been in vain. Robins perch on the fence posts now, and the songs I hear belong to other birds. But it's enough now to know that bluebirds are nearby.

Bluebirds will return to nest in the same area and even choose the same type of nesting site they were born in. When I first read this fact I found it touching, even homey. But this morning it dawns on me what this really means. If a bluebird born in a nest box needs to have a nest box to successfully nest and raise its young, then more nest boxes need to be put up each season.

I go to work. The bluebird box my nephew made years ago in a shop class fell down last winter, and it is still sitting on our front porch bench. I get out the hammer and nail it firmly back to its spot on an old oak. This afternoon I plan to locate some new boxes and put them up in our yard. We have room for at least two on the edge of our field and there's still time for a bluebird pair or two to settle in.

I can't think of a better way to say thank you to the bluebirds for those sure and sustaining thrills.

WATERCRESS

In April I keep a pair of scissors in the glove compartment of my car, along with a plastic bag or two. This time of year I'm always on the lookout for watercress. Midday I pull off Barnes Road and park by the Oak Bluffs waterworks. It's a marvel that this thin causeway marks the crucial divide between salt water and fresh. To my left is the water we drink. To my right is the water we swim in and sail on, the brine that nurtures the clams and oysters and striped bass we eat. Just being here makes me happy. I sit in the car and savor feeling warm and alive in yet another spring.

After a while, I grab the scissors and a bag and make my way around the chainlink fence. The pathway hugs the public water supply, and I pass a couple fishing from an old park bench, though they're more intent on each other than anything else. Soon I reach a fairyland of simmering streams choked with new leaves of cress. No one else is here now, but occasional footprints in the mud remind me that others make this pilgrimage too — including deer, whose hoof prints dimple the wet earth.

Kneeling in the damp, I snip and taste, gradually filling my small bag. I could be done in a minute, but I take my time and move from place to place for the sheer pleasure of it. The new green is so welcome after the long winter that even my knees welcome the wet. A low dead limb makes a perfect seat, so I pause to watch geese pairing up on the sparkling pond and spot a yellow warbler in its nest above me.

Others have left their scissor marks. They are a shared benediction of this season and place, testament to the fact that the cress has returned and so have we. Bag and spirit full, I turn back to my waiting car. Tonight I'll make a salad to honor this place by combining this tangy cress from the reservoir with some bay scallops my husband gathered from the salty side.

Seared Scallops with Watercress
and Warm Orange Dressing

1 large bunch watercress (2 or 3 cups)
2 tablespoons olive oil
Salt and pepper
1 teaspoon light vinegar (Champagne, rice, Moscatel)
1/2 cup diced fresh pineapple
2 radishes, trimmed and very thinly sliced
3/4 pound sea scallops, membranes removed, rinsed and patted dry
[bay scallops may be substituted]
2 lemon wedges

Warm Orange Dressing
Juice of one blood orange or tangerine
1 tablespoon light vinegar
1 teaspoon maple syrup or pinch of sugar

Remove the thicker stems from the watercress and roughly chop the rest of the bunch. In a bowl, toss the watercress with 1 tablespoon of the oil and a pinch or two of salt. Sprinkle with 1 teaspoon vinegar. Place greens on a serving platter or on two individual plates and top with the pineapple and radishes.

Heat a large, heavy skillet over medium-high heat; when hot, add the remaining teaspoon of oil. Sear the scallops for 2 or 3 minutes on each side, taking care to brown each side but not overcook. Sprinkle salt on each side of the scallops during cooking. Remove scallops from the pan and arrange on the salad.

To make the dressing, add the orange or tangerine juice, remaining tablespoon of vinegar, and maple syrup to the same pan, set on high, and bring to a boil. Cook until liquid is slightly reduced and thickened, about 3 or 4 minutes.

Grind some fresh pepper and squeeze a little lemon juice over the salad. Drizzle the sauce over and around the scallops. Serve immediately, while scallops are still hot.

From *Raising the Salad Bar* by Catherine Walthers.

WOMPESKET WALK

This is moving, cleaning, packing, and renting time for many of us Islanders. I am one of them, and I know how easy it is to get caught up in your own clutter and forget how lovely the Island is in early June. Sunday, after too much time in the basement, I needed to get out of the house, take a brisk walk and clear my head.

The parking lot at the beach was full as I drove by, but when I pulled off Lambert's Cove Road into the Blackwater Pond Reservation, no one was there. Once the weather is nice, people can forget how much more than beaches the Vineyard offers. An early-June beach day is an ideal time to explore the late-spring woods. The temperature is just right for walking. At this time of year there are no pesky bugs, and the walker is rewarded by wildflowers in abundance. If it's solitude you need, as I did, there is plenty of it. On a two-hour walk I saw many animals, but not one human.

The trail system here offers a wide variety of walking options. The Land Bank and the Nature Conservancy have done a terrific job of connecting properties and maintaining the trails between them. Whatever your energy level, the wind, or the weather, there is a fine walk to be had. A large map by the parking area will help you outline a route, but some of the fun can be poking around and chancing a little confusion. The worst that can happen is a longer walk.

Sunday I needed a lengthy walk and set my sights on Wompesket, an eighteen-acre gem with a stream and a lovely open meadow. No parking is close to this property and from the various places you can park — Duarte's Pond, Ripley's Field, or Tisbury Meadow — the walk is long. This keeps it remote. I'd been there at least a dozen times and never met another walker.

It was tempting to sit at Duarte's Pond and watch the young Canada goose families, but I was antsy. Crossing the pond on the boardwalk, I paused to look at the wild irises in full bloom before continuing on. Usually I stick close to the Blackwater Ponds, but today I opted for the path that takes you through the woods. I was still running through my lists of things to do, but already I felt better. The trail was lined with starflowers and wild lily of the valley. Catbirds were calling and the sound of a woodpecker hard at work filled the air.

When I got to where the trail ended at a dirt road, I was surprised to be there already. Here the direction can be confusing. Turn to your right and very shortly there will be a trail to your left sign-posted to Wompesket. You'll feel like you are entering a secret world. There are two trails that loop in the shape of an eight. All choices are good ones.

Finally my pace slowed. I watched a pair of mallards in one of the two small ponds and meandered through the meadows noting the location of blooming blueberries for later when their berries would be ripe. A friend told me that blueberry blossoms taste like blueberries. I tried a few and they do. It's a hint, but palpable.

I had been counting varieties of wildflowers, but now I lost count and just enjoyed the sun on a buttercup and the tiny pink blossoms of the wild laurel. My heart stopped when I came upon a cluster of pink lady's slippers. So rare and so beautiful and so fleeting, these flowers thrill me.

After poking around the tiny stream watching frogs, I lost all sense of time. Emptied out, I could turn toward home. Exiting the magic of Wompesket, I took another route back to the parking lot. This trail took me past a pond, along another trail in the Blackwater Pond system and finally along the lovely ponds themselves. My step was light and my energy and focus were on what was right there in that moment. Full circle brought me back to the boardwalk across Duarte's Pond and past the wild iris, but now I could savor them, with my feet firmly on the ground, spirits soaring. The trek had cleaned me out.

RESOURCES

BOOKS

American Heritage Dictionary of the English Language. Second College Edition. Boston, MA: Houghton Mifflin, 1982.

Beard, James. *Beard on Food.* New York, NY: Knopf, 1974.

Bittman, Mark. *How to Cook Everything.* Hoboken, NJ: John Wiley and Sons, 2008.

Carson, Rachel. *Silent Spring.* Boston, MA: Houghton Mifflin, 1962.

Concise Oxford Dictionary: Tenth Edition. New York, NY: Oxford University Press, 1999.

Faulkner, William, *Go Down, Moses.* New York, NY: Random House, 1942.

Flender, William. *Walking Trails of Martha's Vineyard. Fourth Edition.* Martha's Vineyard, MA: Vineyard Conservation Society, 2010.

Hazan, Marcella. *Essentials of Italian Cooking.* New York, NY: Knopf, 2000.

King, Louise Tate and Jean Wexler. *The Martha's Vineyard Cookbook: A Diverse Sampler from a Bountiful Island.* Chester, CT: Globe Pequot Press, 1971.

LaMotte, Richard. *Pure Sea Glass: Discovering Nature's Vanishing Gems.* Chestertown, MD: Chesapeake Seaglass Publishing, 2007.

Mirel, Elizabeth Post. *Plum Crazy: A Book about Beach Plums.* New York, NY: Clarkson N. Potter, Inc, 1973.

Sargent, Robert. *Ruby-Throated Hummingbirds.* Mechanicsburg, PA: Stackpole Books, 1999.

Sibley, David Allen. *The Sibley Guide to Birds.* New York, NY: Knopf, 2000.

The Old Farmer's Almanac. Dublin, NH: Yankee Publishing, 2011.

Walthers, Catherine. *Raising the Salad Bar.* New York, NY: Lake Isle Press, 2007.

Whiting, Susan B. and Barbara B. Pesch. *Vineyard Birds.* Concord, MA: The Massachusetts Audubon Society, 1983.

Whiting Susan B. and Barbara B. Pesch. *Vineyard Birds II.* Edgartown, MA: Vineyard Stories, 2007.

MAGAZINES

Bon Appetit. December, 2007.

WEBSITES

www.allaboutbirds.org
www.hummingbirds.net/map

FARMS

Blackwater Farm
Good Farm
Mermaid Farm
West Tisbury Farmer's Market

WALKS

Blackwater Pond Reservation
Cranberry Acres
Hoft Farm
Ice House Pond (Manaquayak Preserve)
Lambert's Cove Beach
Quansoo
Sepiessa
Wompesket

ACKNOWLEDGEMENTS

I want to thank my dear friend and teaching partner, Barbara O'Neil, and my sister, Snowden Wainwright, for encouraging me to keep writing, and my teachers, Natalie Goldberg and Sally Brady, for always pushing and challenging me. I'm grateful to the editors at the *Martha's Vineyard Times* for publishing many of these essays in an earlier form and to Jan Pogue for listening to my proposal and believing there could be a *Home Bird*. Above all, I want to thank my husband, Whit Griswold, for his careful editing, exacting proofreading, and enduring support.

SUMMARY OF THE ART

The works of art in this book are reproductions of prints that were created with traditional intaglio techniques. The images usually begin as line etchings by warming a mirror-finish copper plate and applying a thin layer of beeswax and asphaltum varnish as a 'resist'. Fine lines are drawn on the plate with a steel needle, exposing the metal beneath. The plate is submerged in an etch solution which corrodes the drawn lines. Stiff, oil-based ink is rubbed into the incised lines, a damp paper is laid over, and the roller of the press transfers the image to the paper. Color is applied as colored ink or in a two-plate process or sometimes as hand-color afterwards.